Perishable World

ISBN 978-1-7364799-1-9
Library of Congress Control Number: 2021934776

Painting (detail) from the author's collection:
Light in the Forest by Pamela Mills
Painting Photograph by Richard Nicol
Cover and Book Design by Lauren Grosskopf

Pleasure Boat Studio books are available
through your favorite bookstore and through the following:
Baker & Taylor, Ingram, Amazon, bn.com &
PLEASURE BOAT STUDIO: A NONPROFIT LITERARY PRESS
PLEASUREBOATSTUDIO.COM
Seattle, Washington

Alicia Hokanson's *Perishable World* is a book of mourning—for the earth, for her parents, for her recently deceased husband. And yet, it is also a rich celebration of all it mourns: most notably the landscape of her island cabin, "Love built this house," on land and a garden with its creatures lovingly detailed—*In these broken days—half the nation whipsawed in grief. . . the sum of autumn's rubric/ is light and color. . . late bees in the penstemon/ still gathering pollen for the hive.* In the stunningly moving poems written after his death, her late husband comes alive: *the tattered chair/ in front of the computer/where you invited every virus/ with your reckless searching.* And in the exquisite poem "Ritual": *this shore where you would /each night exclaim,/ "we are so lucky"* as we, her readers are so lucky to have this fine, overdue collection of an accomplished poet.

—Anne Pitkin, author of *Winter Arguments* and others

"Who knows if the grief I squeeze through my lips can be borne?" says an ancient Aztec singer. In this collection, prize-winning poet Alicia Hokanson sets out to map the raw boundaries of grief by ruthlessly examining occasions and consequences of loss, offset by close and affectionate attention to the smallest nuances of the sensual universe. We learn that what perishes from this world is not only bearable, but inseparable from what we celebrate.

—Samuel Green, former Washington Poet Laureate,
author of *Disturbing the Light*

Perishable World

Alicia Hokanson

PLEASURE BOAT STUDIO: A NONPROFIT LITERARY PRESS

CONTENTS

I.

II.

III.

IV.

for the whole rootball

*

in memory of MPT

I.

Your body is the broker for the wound and the miracle.

—Brenda Hillman

Left on the Porch

polished curve of oyster shell
hidden whorl of whelk

white-striped rocks for wishing on
grey feather abandoned by a gull

flat black shale that fits the thumb
for skipping far

brittle dollars incised with stars
pink cockles and bleached crab claws

summer's piled treasure
gathered from beach walks

emptied from the children's pockets
all these talismans

rimmed now with blown in leaves
fir needles and dust

swept into the bucket for dispersal
down the forest path to the shore

strewn along the tideline
tossed to wave and rip

pummeled in the winter wash
lost in the seasons' wild shuffle

Eurydice, In Winter

Today deep frost on the Field of Asphodel
and the children exclaiming,
It looks just like snow.
I could almost remember excitement like theirs–
that loose fire in the blood.

I watch the ferryman on the black river
struggle to lift coins from mouths of the fallen.
His hands can barely hold them,
but I can see he wants so much to feel
their glittering weight.

In this place everything falls away and falls away–
even the hound patrolling the bank
is only growls and posturing.

Though I have begged the goddess
for some small remnant of my other life,
she cannot help. She is only a cold, pale girl
who misses her mother.

You know what I long for—

notes along the deep chord strung
between breast and thigh,
                    the least pull away a death

if your arm leaves the nest of my side.
What a disturbance
of earth and sky—

until we open our eyes,
gathered back into the world.

Old Love

Begin again with the garden: the visible
squalor of winter—
bare stalks and rumpled leaves.

Begin with widow-planning
when you wake to his coughing,
a cold playing havoc with his ruined lungs.

Begin with the cat, burrowing
under the covers at 5 a.m.,
crying against your chest.

Begin with the morning deck covered in rain
though sun was promised,
a mild January day.

Consider how fate funneled you here
to these woods
opening onto cobbled shore,
to this trampled heart,
this love that moves from exasperation
to storm, to tenderness,
remembering its 30-year prophecy:
standing then in the doorway
of a rented shack, *you are the love
of my life*—
his beautiful, gruff body,
his gold eyes,
sirening you in—
how here, this late afternoon
rain drumming the roof
of the house he built for you
summons a bliss
out of the passion
that once possessed you.

In February

Two books this week, or maybe three, contending
that everything is Nature, even our despoiling of it:
the whole world now our garden, our hands upon it.

In the clearing, yesterday, the rain came down all afternoon
over the lichened apple trees spreading arthritic
fingers into the grass, over the seeds
of maple rooted in the high gutters
trying to grow trees out of the muck
and moss-slid debris on their plastic ledge,
from which the rain, overflowing,
plunked down its harder notes
on the deck, splashing door and siding.

This morning the light moves into day
the way a new-built fire
burns along kindling's edges, burnishing:
the green room of the clearing still and seeping
gold from every opening of branch
or elderberry arch, the alders gilded in round eastern light.

Though no wind ruffles the firs
or cedars, distant waves
are pounding the shore
and light pours from the blue
direction of their roar
where northern mountains burst
the far horizon with new snow.

I watch the light flow over the garden,
imagining the flowering currant's magenta
spindles soon awaiting the rufous's return,
—that wild pink flung into early spring
like a starting flag to draw them
round the earth curve home to its nectars—

and the light glides over the climbing rose
in its stiff thorns, over gentle clematis
unwinding its next length of leaf,
and the peony's maroon unfurling,
staunch in its circle of new soil:
the light itself imagining
a June of staggering blossoms—

May: Metaphysical Inbox

Morning's fog in the evergreens,
thin as the lining of a dream.

Grey brightens to bluish white,
becoming faint shapes of clouds.

Out of such stillness: the gleaming day.
Bees hum in the soft blur of the apple tree.

Purple-blue spikes of ajuga ramble
all through the garden like the syllables

gathering color in my mouth: anemone,
yarrow, nasturtium, mint.

The hand is a rake, the foot a hoe;
the hip is a bending hinge.

Burn pile tended to ashes, the new-mown
field and its scythed edges:

here dwells the human will—
our brief, happy hubris.

Sitting with Iris

Charmed one, flower of summer,
weary of being passed arm to arm,
she comes to my lap on the bench
where late June sun is spreading shadows
around the goldfish pond.

I whisper to her the litany of what's before us:
a junco hopping in Indian plum,
dragonfly darting for mosquitoes,
the black cat slinking toward the rocks,
the old dog circling in the brown shade
of rhododendrons.
How the hush of evening settles us.

Sucking her fingers softly,
she leans against me
and we watch the dusk come on
in the lush, almost-twilight
breath of the late day
in this creatured world
her new soul is coming to know.

Commonwealth

stillness is the morning's dress:
thin white netting of clouds
overlaid on blue sky, green boughs

a little ruching of light
on the cedars' trunks,
row of white fir stitching
the understory

coolness on the woods' trail,
the mossy path opening
to the beach's bright arena

small boats pulled above the tide line
sea salt smell
                        eagle shadow passing over
tutelary spirit
from sand flats to rocky point

across the bay, kayakers
make quick progress, one blue
one yellow, voices rise then fade
moving east,

trailing wind
riffles on the water

panorama of sea and islands
Canada north, humped Saturna
rising from the haze

a family of otters' sinuous
curves in the bay, undulating light

childhood's landscape and dream
memory's gauzy dress

Outer Island Journal

towhees rustle in salal,
mining richness in the margins

my body loose in summer jeans
pushing back the clearing

with machete and mattock,
whacking down elderberry, thorny currant

through songbird calls in the thicket
looking for the well site

—

sunrise through woods a gold glowing
bright shafts of blue
that are the sea beyond:

a dark blue rip churns strong past Bare Rock
while the Bonaparte gulls wheel against
the green flanks of Saturna

two crows preen and peck at the water's edge

hazy mountains north, indigo patches of riptide,
and all the colors of tide-washed stones

—

worshipped also the dark grey, dark
green god of winter

the stillness of forest roads
dampened by fir needles, wind-blown fronds

surrounded by the gods of cedar
their wavering, bending, upright glory

loved most the winter's night,
an inner kingdom opening:
those fiery islands of the dark

I hear death walk down the years—

a rain that goes on falling
in slow, quiet veils

—

winter's stillness descends
in the drizzle of this grey coast

burn-pile smoke drifts into the yard
hangs over the abandoned garden

evening slips its perfect darkness down
onto the house moored between

a wet and brooding forest
and the grey swell of sea

—

islanded by stove and lamplight
some days the loud distress of so much silence

an owl flies out of the rain
into the woods   and then the rain

comes down again

a sharp green sound

—

dust of summer roads dampening
the sheen of ditch weeds,

bike tires plumping over stones,
my shoulders pulled by the backpack
full of books I borrowed

I'm stopped by the sky
over Adams' field—

glow of palest peach
behind rows of dark firs,

the still grasses giving up
their color to the night

—

light wind and evening coolness
light wind that is evening's courier

as if to name the weather
were to name these muffled longings

lifted on blue swells
kayaking into a neon sunset:

groan of sea lions out past Skipjack,
bobbing skull of the sentinel seal—

At Griffin Bay

Splayed white knobs on spiky arms,
starfish, orange and maroon,
            and swaying green
    tentacles
            of urchin and anemone
      stained the tidepools clear through
               with color—

A diamond net glistened there
            stretching to incandescent
               mosses on the hillside
      and to small grasses
         waving in the sun

      (each stem a thread
      vivacious with its underlife)

      that wove us
         to the sea billowing
            under the blue weft of sky.

But I had learned Heaven
      was an afterlife

      and could not throw off the mind
      to become
      color   shape   sun
        sea   cloud   tide

Listening to the Sea at Point Wilson

Hardly a way to say it: the *ssshhlip* and *ngelunk,*
the *splush*—a grayer sound
foams in the lip of the tide.
Waves fall over themselves with no wind
pushing them up the beach,
shimmer on sand and fade.

Irregular curves cut sand the way
the cry of gulls scallops the air
above the herring ball. Their bodies
rise and drop–a teeter-totter of birds–
dark edges of wings V-ing. Beyond them
the resonant R's of small planes over firs.

Wind makes no sound today, is only felt
in the silken drift of hair across a cheek.
The tongue, too, rests.
In the fruitless cave of the mouth
the river slips underground.

No words for the sound of waves
or the curve inside their breaking.

In the Vale of Soul-making

—Keats

Cloud-cobbled sky
and pine-layered hillside
against the absolute
stillness of daybreak.

Stellar's jay hops along the deck,
peering at the sleeper
curled in her bag.

The hourglass drifts across my blue screen—
four wireless systems are detected (one unsecured).
I am unsecured in my heart today, but won't

fall into despair, for there are still words
to be found for the radiant specifics:
one struck against another, flaming.

At lift-off our small plane banked
over the wrinkled skin of summer waters
glittering below. The old, old sea—
which is every day renewed.

The same tasks address you.
The 22,000 days of your life unroll behind
and the work ahead bequeathed:
muddle and shine—
no other world but this.

Beauty Resists

So unexpected to come upon it
as we followed the swerving
waxwings, their commotion
in the air our umbrellas curtained:

the gold Gingko
—double trunk rising
from its yellow leavings—
paving the sidewalk
with real luster,
cement softer under the mash
of ochre leaves along the gutters.
Shine of rain over everything.

In the park, vine maples hold on
to some crimson tatters
above the banks where the last salmon
fight their way home
in the stream bed
the neighbors made good again.

In these broken days—
half the nation whipsawed in grief
at what we will become—
the sum of autumn's rubric
is light and color in the trees,
flash of silver fins in the creek,

and late bees in the penstemon
still gathering pollen for the hive.

Credo

I believe in the forest's stillness
and in the wood beetles' work:
random *thunk* of the eaten branch

in the raven's rasp
and the jangle of crows in a gnarled plum
calling up the morning

in the edges of clearings:
their gold thirst where light slips in

in the persistence of blackberry—
roots out of rock in the glaciered soil,
unfurling sweetness in the knobs of their making

in the grace of the cat—hummingbird leaper,
beach-path prancer, crier in the salal—
I am her adored one

I believe in the tide, architect of sand and cobble
masking and unmasking a new beach each day

in sleep, country of night composed
of memory and desire, weaving the day's
small notes through a larger drama

I believe in the surge of dark-blue rip
churning strong past Skipjack,
and in the steady gulls riding the edge

To T'ao Chi'en

No pony ride through mountains—I've travelled ragged
highways with sixteen-ton trucks—to reach this soli-
tude,

where northern mountains rise beyond a grey sea,
empty trails winding to peaks that touch the sky.

My rivers run in tides, ridden by gulls
and drift logs swirled past buoys.

Though my cabin's not made of rushes
and my metal roof is guaranteed to last a hundred years,

I, too, watch the ten thousand things
swirl, dance, die, and rise—

the peony's red crown
holds the rain-soaked soil,

rusted stalks still held
by spring's green ties.

II.

Not quite dark yet
and the stars shining
above the withered fields

—Buson

Scars

one small red arc over
my right breast where
the surgeon carved
the lump out

its twin hidden
under the arm where
she pulled a stringy sack

out, left a numbness
a twitch and burn

and the body

the body has to go

into that silence
where all voices start

and live

Fierce

painted all Kwakiutl blues
and blacks, raven wings,
soul-country greens,
slipping out of the swamp
dark forest dream

go deeper said the puppet man

I want back into the beginning,
flying the rusted hulk of a car,
a cloud-split sky
breaking blue around me

this is the journey
its dark teachers

wind rakes the trees and rain
beats into the ice blackened street
already I wonder who will want
my books, my shoes,
the blue cloth journals

oh call me back
to the calm
of the moment's duty
being *here*
before non-being is born

October Nocturne

How shall the heart be reconciled
to its feast of losses....
> —Stanley Kunitz

1

A week ago my uncle played
quick measures of Chopin,
asking me how the piano sounded.
So beautiful! I told him
To me it is the rattling of tin cans, he said.
He can't hear the overtones—the music
doesn't reach inside him anymore.

Trying to do the crosswords together,
my voice squawking through his hearing aid
as he strains to puzzle out the clues,
he's distracted by the perfect blush
of pink in the heart of the bouquet
of yellow alstroemeria—

His eyes grow blurry,
even the heavy magnifier
doesn't make the pages clear.
At dinner, he drifts into sudden sleep
as autumn sun makes prisms
of the thinning leaves.

2

Under the bruised dusk
of the horizon's jagged mountains,
one small mast light blinks
adrift on twilight sea,
as I drive to take up again
the vigil by his bed.

Slipping a Bach CD
into the dashboard slot,
all the melancholy nights
pour out—his piano calling up
my childhood:

the living room hushed,
we watch his fingers' impossible
dance among the notes.
Jesu, Joy of Man's Desiring—
his mother's favorite.
All my aunts are tearing up.
My heart is the muffled felt
of hammers on the keys.

3
Behind his apartment, 3:00 a.m.,
sirens ring up and down the avenue
where in his boyhood trolleys ran,
and city lights blink and shine
across the hillsides and downtown.

I sit in the bedroom
changing the music,
as he becomes a child again
moaning when we move him
to change the cloths, straighten
the pillows and the sheets.

I slip another syringe past his tongue
struggling against the silence.

As the sonata resolves, note
by slowing note, open-mouthed,
his breath sustains the chord
connecting him to us,

and he who said
I don't recommend living past 100
holds on,
not finished yet
with Earth.

in memory,
Randolph Hokanson, 1915-2018

BLUE BARDO SUITE

Alongside Her Dying

The courtyard Buddha sits before the light
fringe of white alyssum in dim November.

Let their frayed ruffles stand
for what fades from life these mornings,

as though Persephone had gathered
their blooms to strew downriver,

the first grey clouds
like something torn from her hem.

In the vault of morning, memory strays
as juncos do, rummaging dry stalks of peonies.

Windy gusts drive pellets of rain
through the disheveled day.

Rain tries all the windows,
pounds at the lintels,

while grief picks the locks,
slips in without knocking.

November Fragments

Sick
of the leg spasms
of the unbalanced
lift and swing, she worries

the hot red lump on her hand
where the needle stuck.

One eye opens, a tear
pooling in its corner.

Where do you travel, wayfarer,
in those dreams that panic you?

After a two-hour nap, still
exhausted, I try visualizing
a radiance pouring over her,
saints and buddhas hovering,
urging her soul toward light.

If that's what souls do—
I want to believe those tough old Tibetans,
and the deep peace of Rilke's poems
is nearly convincing.

Today's bardo is rain, grey light
weightless as the cat's speckled eye upon me.

Burble of the oxygen machine.
Soup spills blended into the colors of her shirt.
You should write this story, she says.

Last Words

At lunch, Mother wants
to make an announcement,
banging the spoons
do they understand what's going on?
banging the spoons on the white tablecloth
listen listen listen

the grey sky lowers itself again
over the rained-in city
over the harbor's orange cranes

out her window: the bare maple's
knuckled branches curl back on themselves

bent from the hip repair, her leg
locks into its shrunken curve
as her cries *helpme helpme*
omygod
lock like a needle,
after the song has played out,
sticks against a crack in black vinyl

trapped in the shrinking world
of her bed and the terrifying sling,
next to the waiting wheelchair's black seat,
she pushes away the tray—
where am I?

The nurse brings morphine.
Atropine,
for congestion in the throat,
I know must come
from *Atropos:* her shears
that cut life's thread
as the mind winds down to chaos

to the mad, stuck beat of her chant
to her half-opened eye
to silence

In the Nursing Center

The small, blue birds on her hospital gown—
poor joke—they fly all over her.
Pentecostal bird in the Sunday missal,
birds like blue gulls fly
over tides of tears that wash us—

driving the black fissures
of rain-slick streets,
or traveling through the light
of stripped branches,
in gusts of wind blowing through
interstices of grief or remembered joy.

Whoosh of the oxygen machine.
Her warm hands. Her sleep of Morpheus.

What fragments of red wind,
what infernos of loss
blow through her now?

On her fevered forehead
the green washcloth is folded at the edges
like some Tibetan hat.

From her opened lips, dry breaths
still move in tidal rhythm,
force of earth's body.

When the white light of the mind descends
and the red force rises up
to meet at the heart center,
the Buddhists say, then the soul may leave—

O mystery   O wayfarer, suffering
do not linger here—

Last Lesson

her eyes, blue glass,
open wide

two gasps,
a small jerk of her head

a low moan
as teeth and tongue let go

an animal shudder
and slackening

the head lolls
then the sightless eye:

feral
and complete

her face
a yellow husk of skin

I tried to do the *phowa:*
come all you saints all you buddhas

mother mary jesus christ
come to her now

comfort her fears
carry her to the luminosity

that she may know her mind
enlightened

and then the aides, the nurse,
my sisters, and the hospice social worker:

sudden flurry of activity—
gather the photos,

clean out the drawers,
unsling her clothes from the closet

in memoriam, MFH 1920 - 2012

Evening Walk

trampled leaves and grass
moist on the beach path:
fragrance of sweet
autumn decay

high tide's weed-swirl
floating the drift logs
at the marsh's edge

sky color is wave color
grey/blue/grey/blue

then sumi ink clouds
over water white
in sundown glare

stillness settling in
like the ferns fanned
wide into the trail

and the question mark
calls of wrens
in the elderberries

evening's moth hovers
above still waters
where the grey light
is leaving us

Teaching Homer to Eighth Graders

What appeals to them most is that Odysseus
was one horny guy
moving from goddess to nymph;
not that he kept his vision
of Ithaca like a flame in his gut.

And Telemachus—that wimp—
turned out to be okay,
he could have strung the bow
if his dad had let him.

Argos, on the dung heap, rolls
his eyes and dies,
joy in his doggy heart
when he hears his master's voice.

And Eurylochus
—a fool to eat those cattle—
got what he deserved.

Nausicaa? An idiot
to let a naked man
from the bushes by the river
nearly hug her about the knees.

With what glee they read
the bloody battle in the hall.
How cool that Antinous
got it in the throat
and that Melanthius
was strung up on a brutal wall.

How far we've come
when they begin to feel
the complications of return

to greening Ithaca,
and kneel in the orchard
with Laertes weeping.

The old guy fooled
by a son just beginning
the shipwrecked journey home.

Father

You said, *There are so many white butterflies
up there,* pointing
to ascending limbs of fir trees
and the moths we could see
fluttering there in afternoon light.

I wanted to know what pain
you hid from us, the interior
life you kept.

I think I know that inward turning
others read as rejection
when we are only trying
to come to ourselves—

As on a July afternoon
white moths gather
in the cool, high branches
of the firs.

Spark

On his journey, Odysseus becomes *Nobody,*
almost nameless to the Phaeacians who
have promised passage home, where he's transformed
to a beggar in his own kingdom—

Some days I think maybe the old shouldn't teach the young.
What hope have I to offer them, so newly tuned
to the world, while I am monitoring its decay?
Grey lichen on the plum's spindly limbs grows
like gnarled fists. Arthritic fingers of the apple tree
reach far into the grass.

So many questions trace a path through
my students' hearts–why we care what others say,
where we get the courage to be
unique, cranky, imperfect, glorious—
They are coming to own themselves.
They want to save the Earth.

Today, my father totters, falls, and falls again
from his regal bearing to a slack, bent back
dotted with brown spots and the bruises
of his knocking about at 90: water
on the elbow, lump above the eye
where the shower rod hit him going down—

The students have written their poems in chalk
outside on the pathway for the rain to use.

New Shades

Because at late winter sundown
the light hits his eyes so brightly,
we're putting up new shades
in my father's bedroom.

Through the window, freighters
glide past the city, past the mountain
gathering its silence.

Yet the view he loved all his life
does not tell him this is home.
Some other place entices.
He asks each visitor,
Did you bring a car?

Soon he'll walk
the Field of Asphodel
with Hector and Achilles,
speaking of honor among the heroes

and in the great court
with Rhadamanthus
debate the finer points
of death's law.

Last Day

I had risen from my bed
where, in my half sleep, you came to me:
dapper in your fine suit coat and fedora,
smiling, home from court,
my childhood father,
tower of certainty in all the trembling world.

You were not the old man fading in that blue room,
your eyes searching upward,
your tongue a dark petal in red wind.

We sat with you and heard your lungs
labor past the rattle in your throat

held your hands
(fingers still fine and smooth),

watched you move
from breath to breath

while the day blew
gusty, rain-driven
with sudden dazzles of sun
over your cherry trees bursting with light—

Mind Over Matter

—Kept waking along the edge of utterance
silence was pushing words forward
and the ledge was steep

—Say *grief* and the shoulders hunch
say it for a long time and your cells may speak it
sprout a dark node near your heart

—Poplars at sunset waving and fluttering:
the ballast of matter shifting
against the thin hull of the sky

—Across the bay the loon's cry
slips from the striped cage of its throat

Obit

He was an aria sung in the shower,
steel of those blue-grey eyes,
a suit coat, tie and fedora.
He was the law in the four-story house.

He was philosophy, history, and art,
Latin and a little Greek,
Sunday morning's Beethoven and Bach.
He was writing briefs long into the dark.

He was a six-day working week,
an argument we couldn't win,
the words and what they mean.
He was the mold he made us in.

He was a straw boater and a seersucker suit,
the rowboat and hooked bullheads,
sets of tennis and a strong golf swing.
He was gin and tonic by the beach.

He was Librium in the shaving kit,
a morose Swede he joked,
another strange word we didn't know.
He was a hard love to show.

He was a dented, blue Mercedes,
daily bruises and Coumadin skin,
a stuttering heart's new valve.
He was a memory starting to slow.

He was dividend checks uncashed.
Asleep in the pool of midnight lamp,
he was a vanquished and open heart
holding the words and what they mean.

in memoriam, RVH 1913 - 2007

III.

Who's learned to see through this perishable world?

—Mountain poems of Stonehouse (Shih-wu)
translated by Red Pine

Fulcrum

A sliver in the plank that hangs
over the balance point, you
want to believe it is enough to *see*
such wild strangeness:
spotted autumn spiders' quiet

webs in the yard everywhere, blue
patterns of brown and grey
in the tomcat's fur, scent of cedar,
fire in the leaves, fire

in the hearth beating back the dark
and the strange comfort in being
of that dark which nightly drops
black clues to the implacable center—
the pivot on which your board tilts.

In the dream you braced your feet
against the police-station counter
and screamed for the battered earth
with such frenzied anger and sorrow
they let you go on your own recognizance.

World Without Us

No one has told the gulls
the human world is doomed:
they scrabble loudly over the herring ball
roiling in the sun. But those two crows
crying as they strut the tideline this afternoon
give a piercing, inconsolable moan.

The sun doesn't know, nor the tide,
or the big combers rolling in to take out
the fire ring rocks, flatten the beach,
and rearrange the logs. They will keep
thrashing the shore long after we are gone,
when the sea has moved a hundred feet up
into the trees and carved out a newer island.

Who will miss our loud machines
and brutal histories? Will anything miss
our beach chairs and the shouts of children
playing in the shallows? Our tended gardens
and tamped roads connecting house to house?

The wrens in summer thickets will still
be here. And morning's stillness, I hope.

What of our words? Our small, thin songs
of praise or love? Leave them
to the whales. I hope the whales go on
carrying this longing through the deep
watery canyons of the world.
And for the shore, the crow's dark lament.

In a Blue State

After the campaign,
the multiple despairs,
the rift down the middle
of the map, angry polemics
on the Facebook pages,
free floating anxiety
and its sleepless nights,

I read in today's paper
that psychologists counsel
self care: try laughter,
a long walk,
a return to your art.

Gather friends,
play music and turn
off your devices—
find your way back to living
in the local wonders.

Autumn is still fanning
gold flames in the gardens;
waxwings swerve
and swoop before us,
drunk on the abundance
of the rowan's red berries.

We step through the rain
onto the bright paths
of maple and gingko
spreading rust and scarlet
across the neighborhood street.

The bookstore fills
the small white space
with poets
and their friends:
a transforming music.

And after,
Were the poems too sad?
she asks.

I say, *The world
is too sad,
but you still need to tell it—*

as Emily, on her journey,
left small packets tied with ribbon.

And the lichens you studied
in their chemical revolution
sometimes take centuries
to break the granite.

for BH

Our Paradise

In the dusty schoolyard, after the geologist's talk
    (upthrust of folded rock
    carved hidden harbors,
    these islands made beautiful
    by fault lines of basalt),
my neighbor and I discuss human nature.

I tell him we are a species grown unfit for the planet
which will soon shrug us off with the same disdain
as when the red ants swarmed up from scrap wood
I was tossing from the yard, and I shook them off
with a flick of my ankle *(O, what a piece of work is man),*
but he was passionate
that we can be taught
and we can change.

The morning news, the evening news, tell of greed
at the core, some tyranny in us. In America
we turn off the radio and walk to the beach.

Though the sea grows emptier (crab-pot buoys
strung across the bay), and no salmon leap
along the shore, summer's beauty is not yet undone.

Pleasure boaters are few, in this shaky economy,
so the empty shore, these glistening waters, are only ours;
until the unmarked black helicopters
buzz the treetops
cameras at the open door—

Side by Side

*In forms of life other than human, there is a vitality
that isn't trapped in the sorrow.*
—Brenda Hillman

all around the clearing
summer's gold fuse firing the alders

the click and sway of juncos
gliding to grass-light
under apple trees

first heat from the wood
stove kindled to flame;
coffee in the blue cup

while the radio reports
police have shot
another child armed
only with his blackness,

and refugees spilling
from flimsy boats
mass at ragged borders

hummingbirds buzz
the closed blooms of honeysuckle
twining the porch rail

on the trail to the beach:
kingfisher poised on his low branch
chatters before the dive

walking barefoot along the low tide's
selvage, where creamy foam
wreathes our ankles,

the only footprints on the beach
the ones we are making,
that the sea dissolves
as if we had never been

At Anini Beach

Blue water stretches the horizon's curve—
    a fringe of breakers
        foams at the reef's edge,
lifts the eye to the folded hills:
    Namolokama,
        Mamalohoa,

their green flanks holding back
an armada of white clouds.

In my hand, four bars on the cell
connect me to the day's
disasters—the masters of oil
will rule the nation, pipelines
eviscerate the heartland's
prairie, while arctic ice
withers in the winter's heat.

It's so hard to believe in the end
of beauty here—
in warmth and fragrance,
and the eye's pleasure in every direction:
    wild roosters strut
        among the striped towels
        and beach chairs,
sparrows begging scraps
get the half peanut
    fallen to the sand,
black crabs scuttle over lava stones,
tumbled at the end of the bay.

And the sea's unstoppable glistening,
    holds sway in the tender air.

In the Anthropocene

(in memory—Sam Hamill, 1943-2018)

Winter doubles down
on spring, slaps fists of rain
against the marchers

who take to cold streets
and chant, their signs
laminated against

the damp. Some carry
slogans written on umbrellas:
Science not Silence.

In the march of ecocide,
the small subtractions
(one poet's death)

loom larger
in the scheme of things,
where such a voice

could wake us
before we drown.

*In the great
not-knowing
there is only the learning,
the path,
the Way.*

You brought those ancient
poems across the centuries
to show us our time

and place—rain-filled
mountains and rivers
without end—

part of a continuum
we cannot rip,
though we have tried.

The Iceman

...a man older than the pyramids
who walked the Alps before Buddha or Christ,
before Aristotle or Plato....
                              —PBS documentary

Taken by ice and given back,
he came to us whole and we broke him,
looking for our past
stashed in his woven bags
and boots lined with grass,
etched in a bow of yew
or arrows of swift viburnum.

Another gone down on the dark journey
and returned with treasure:
sloe berries ripe with autumn sun,
news of places where earth gives up
its sharpest flint, or a meadow
of curative mushrooms far up the mountainside.

Did he pray to a goddess of snow or fire?
To some Vulcan of copper who blessed his axe?
As the storm overtook him
did he cry out for wife and daughter
weaving reeds for their roof by the lakeshore?

Unburied by his tribe, unburnt, unhallowed,
skin shriveled brown, his fingers curve
with blackened nails. The crust
around his hollowed eyes articulates
the centuries' slow speech
of glaciers, blue quiet of alpine skies.

        Behind his knees, the skin's tattooed
        with hexagrams for wildness and protection.

Snap

30 feet from the house, the double cedar
soaking up our morning sun
and shading out the berries in the yard
has to come down.
Each year the greedy limbs take more
of our abbreviated light.

The crew is trained and hardy,
has all the tools and the machines:
the chipper, picker, the small backhoe
for moving logs and cleaning up
the mess of bark and branches.

Craig shinnies up the southern side
where the trunk splits into two,
and he rigs the cable to pull it back
exactly where they want it to go.
No problem. The chainsaw bites and growls,
the tree teeters and then the sure *thump*
to earth, slow enough to watch it fall.

The other trunk leans north
but cable-tied, they say they'll fell it
south as well, and carefully
he wedges the undercut,
carefully ropes up and balances,
7 feet off the ground
he makes his back-cut true.

Standing around to watch, all of us
are listening for the *whump*
of tree hitting ground
and the stunned silence after.
My camera aims at the bed of needles
where he'll lay it, adjusting the angle
as the whine grows louder.

And then the slender hinge
or inner rot or some hand
of fate takes hold—
the second trunk spins
90 degrees toward home,
the curving branches sweeping down
the face of our house, taking out
every gutter and downspout on the way.

Stunned, we jump and then we run
around the front to see what the tree has done:
no window crack or dented roof,
only some residue of dust along the shingles,
only the gutters down and not the house
crushed by a 90-foot tree. What miracle,
what grace saves us—those supple
limbs of cedar bending
instead of breaking as Doug fir would do?
Even the cable, still attached,
has swung over the roof and missed
solar panels, chimney, vents.

The crew stands an hour trying to read
the hieroglyphics of the stump:
how deep the undercut, how thin
the hinge, how rotten the core.
Or did a small gust of wind
on this cloudless day tip it?

We snap the pictures,
marvel at the light
flooding our new clearing,
alive
to the altered view.

The Grounding Line

Cedars drop their yellowed fronds
and the forest crackles underfoot.
The sturdy ferns collapse
under roadside dust
as sun rises orange in haze and smoke
from northern fires. Unrelenting
heat in June saps the refuge
from even this remote beach.
News of storms and fires and acidic seas
dries out the heart a little more each day.

Antarctic glaciers retreating fast
at the grounding line
detach and begin to float, the ice sheet
melting into the amplitude of tides,
into diminishing returns, the inevitable
sea level rise in meters,
in meters over the coming years.

Flying over Canada, with a god's-eye view
I looked through the cloudless
blue, down to the shores of Hudson's Bay
and saw it as a warm Riviera someday,
and Greenland's icy slabs
fingering into the Atlantic
grew greener under their frosted glaze.

Now late August rain
blown in on unseasonable storms
has drenched our island's soil
and washed away the dust.

Each morning the yellowing maples
brighten a little more in the dew.
The ferns lift their spiky greens
above the soaked moss floor.

Even in the heart of the disaster,
the forest keeps trying
its one unassailable word:
renew.

Since May

The bees fly into the soffit space
above the front door where they
are making a shelter of honeycomb.

Each trip from the garden—from the red jangle
of penstemon, white mouth of rockrose—
their soft gold vibrates with announcing buzz.

They don't bother me going in or out at evening
or early afternoon. They harbor my house
for honey, as I hope they will

when it crumbles in the aftermath
of the human. I don't begrudge them—
small warriors of the old ways.

One Way or Another

As morning slips its light
beneath the blackout shades
and the day moon floats
above the fence,
a gauzy shadow of itself,
I rise to consciousness
with the image of the calving glacier
roiling and melting
into a black sea—

They say it was the size
of Manhattan's island
only taller and all at once—
that loss portending what
will soon become personal, political.

Yesterday, through rain squalls and sun bites
we sped up the freeway after the rock recital:
our granddaughter, nine,
in sequined black jeans
channeling Blondie:

> *One way or another*
> *I'm gonna getcha getcha getcha*

electric red guitar
slung aside as she grabs the mic
and pitches it to us—

Later, reading Mowgli stories to her
as she collapsed, exhausted, in my lap,
her sister, ear-budded and screen-glued,
tells me, *Books now are boring.*

Rebellion is her current ploy
against being second-born. And I see
the coming world colliding already
with our stunned allegiance to the known—

One way or another I'm gonna lose ya
I'm gonna give you the slip

Reply to Shih-wu

> *"Who's learned to see through this perishable world?"*
> —Mountain poems of Stonehouse (Shih-wu)

The sky is clear enough July mornings
to see each fir needle at the branch tips
thrust against the blue.

Grown thick in the moist spring, tall daisies
spill near the wall of the garden shed
holding all of summer's brightness.

Empty beach at 6 a.m: heavy dew drips
from the beach chair slats. Low tide
laps a green seaweed fringe.

Last night, my granddaughter, in love with the mirror,
put on makeup for the beach, shaved her legs
"for pictures" her friends might take.

Around the beach fire the girls debated favorite
shades of eye shadow and brands of gloss,
they whose beauty is wholly undiluted.

This morning of the world: light from the east
shines on nasturtium leaves big as lily pads
flowing down the pot to drape the weathered deck.

Letter from the Island

The light at 5 a.m., mid-July, is almost full. What was
a frail glow quickly brightening. The firs are sentries
of silence, a quarter moon curves white near the top
of the closest cedar. On the high windowsill
the cats are going crazy watching sparrows in the thickets
below where the seep of sun kindles the clearing's edges.

Finally, a real summer day after weeks of rain.
I still don't know how to feel about my luck being here —
sea, sky, beach and woods, fresh raspberries at the farm stand,
blueberries at the U-pick, the bounty of the island
and its seeming safety. How do I hold this gratitude next to
the sorrow and rage? The virus surges; the arctic is burning.

Loggers have moved into the nearby woods.
Like giant hornets in the distance, their machines start up
the droning. A grinding roar winds through the sky.
Yesterday we walked a forest road bordering that hunger
to destroy. My neighbor says it is just the old boys' club —
it's what you do if you have woods — cut them down.
A world of quick wrens and curving boughs for 100 dollars
a thousand board feet, numbers on a ledger that pencils out
to someone's slim profit.

This morning in *The Post* a young writer in Hong Kong
laments the new law that makes dissent a crime
and what it will mean to her city, to her friends — artists,
activists. I think it is time we all lie down with them
in the streets to save ourselves and the earth.
I remember my friend Peter telling me 30 years ago
that the planet would be better off without us.   And yet—

Last evening, I gave Iris her first kayak lesson on the silvering
pre-sunset water, the tide at slack, the bay a bowl of light.
She took to it quickly, finding the balance, but soon tired.
Her thin arms weaken lifting a long paddle, though her legs are strong.
I can't imagine what strength she'll need to survive this life.
She spent the late evening working a colored pencil drawing
of a sunset that glows off the page. Then she took up again
her newest work: affixing a line of fine blue beads
along the edge of a white clam shell.

Gathering

1

At equinox, the slant of light changes
but keeps its strict appointment: seven to seven.
Brilliant days still hooked to summer
come edged in cold and shadows
that cover half the beach.

Fall raises the curtain
on the losses to come, as crackled leaves
curling along the grapevine
crumble into the flax and lithodora.
The cats bat them across the withered lawn
where walking brings gold spiders down.

And summer's toll keeps piling in my heart:
my first lover dead from ALS; a dearest friend
gutted by pain, gone by her own hand;
my love three weeks adrift in hospital beds;
our nation's fabric fraying at the edges—

And now the doctors in their crisp shirts
have said the radiation didn't work, the tumor
grows, and soon our beloved uncle will need
all our care to help him to the door.

2

Carrying her dead calf
the mother orca follows the pod,
lifting the body
up to trailing whale boats,
tourists, helicopters—
      to our sight-seeing push,
      our engine clatter,
      our pollutants filling the waters—

She bears her calf for 16 days,
for a thousand miles,
up into the human world
crying   *this, this* —
She is our activist
in grief and rage
carrying a dying planet
on her rostrum—

3
September coals fall to ash
in the creaking stove, and the days
are measured out in chores:

I've gathered five bins of apples to the press,
two dozen jars of cider canned,
and still one tree's so laden
I can't pick them all myself.

I've gathered, too, some sunsets
burning a fierce horizon,

gathered in a full moon washing
squares of light across the floor,

gathered morning fog in the clearing
to store this forest silence
for our darkening time.

Toward Solstice

The light slides
grey above the trees,
hesitates in the tips of firs,
    (there was once a forest here),
brightens with the stippling rain
on porch and roof.

Surely you have watched
these winter mornings dawn—
your heart scoured out
with grief, after a sleep-starved
night, waking again
to the corrupted wave
that has broken your country.

Hunched crows hold the power
lines above the wet street.

Yet, you are warm in your bed.
Your love dreams beside you.
Morning's minuet plays against the glass.

The courtyard Buddha
wears so lightly his mantle of mist.

Bladed leaves of the rhododendron
swell and shine.

Soon the planet will turn again
in the star-strewn dark
bearing its cargo of hope.

Eclipsed

1

Australia, 1975, on a spring evening
coming home from a night at the pub
with my teaching colleagues, I found,
propelled to the porch light,
some insect hatch—
a twitching pile of pale, brown husks
blocking the door, a mass
still clinging to the screens.
Inside, the kitchen floor was littered
with hundreds of piled rinds.
Took a broom and swept the rasp
of small hard shells along the linoleum.
The utter abundance of them—
all in one evening alive and perishing.

Now the insects are disappearing.
In Holland, the naturalist notices the strange
sensation of a June bike ride with no wings
battering his glasses or stuck against his teeth.
Nothing to spit. A great blankness in the air.

2

The heart traffics in morning's dark
specific grief—this scratched plexiglass
between the feelings and the fear.

Our friend, on her second round with chemo,
has sent a book, *Making Friends with Death.*
The blur on the horizon, my uncle called it.

I sleep. I cook. I can't summon the energy
to clean the house, though I can try to do the kitchen.
These tasks I do today for you, tomorrow I will do alone.

3
Leaving the play,
we watch
this January night,
in a cloudless sky,
the blood wolf moon
ascend the dark
above the theater—
fully eclipsed
improbably red,
suspended
through
rimed winter branches.

IV.

We were born to escort the dead,
and be escorted ourselves.

—Charles Wright

Blueprint

I've found that favorite photograph of you—
your face shadowed against the plywood
of a wall you've just raised:

bare-chested, hammer in hand,
jeans powdered with fresh sawdust,
you lean against the studs,
your bitterness dissolving in good
work, in building something wholly new.

This refuge carved out of time,
out of fir and moss
in the clearing of an abandoned orchard:
agate light, eagle feather,
sea breeze from the north—
our house in sunlit woods.

Those years of building were your therapy.
Jumble of tools after each day's work,
my cleanup job. Under this roof
we hold each other's histories.

Now you tremble on your cane,
and the long bandage of your grief
unwinds itself from the bone.

Reunion

Manzanita, Oregon

Ocean waves wash in without ceasing,
curl and break—sunlit blue
or greyed out in the rain,
they collapse on themselves
and dissolve in thin foam on the beach.

It's easy to let them be background noise,
enjoy the wide view without really feeling
their unrelenting pulse pummel the shore.

In the goodbye bear hug
from your dear nephew
suddenly the tears press out.

Why is it only in the kindness of others
that this grief rises to the surface?

A glance, a hand squeeze,
that more-than-expected embrace
from your young oncologist
catches me out, and I am pulled
into the undertow.

In the sweetness of this gathering—
your children and grandchildren,
your siblings, your nephews,
the whole rootball
of ex-wives, half-brothers, near sisters—
it seems no one but me
shies away from a straight-on look
at your coming death,
though all week the sea
has chanted it in my ear.

Vanish

Is everything going away now

you asked your son
on the day before.

Dozing and sleeping,
you didn't say much else

I pressed your hand,
whispered *thank you—*

for what?
you asked, confused

for our life—

—

sorting pictures
by your bed,
in the coma quiet
I heard the sudden change
in your breath—
the halting gasp

called your son and
your daughter over

the three of us
held on
to you as if
we could keep you
here

—
had to call the hospice nurse
and then

all afternoon you lay
waxen still
while we waited for the van

—
I look for you
in the places you once
lingered—

the stool by the fireplace
where you took your morning smoke
coaxing the grey vapors
up the chimney

your place at the table
requisitioned now by the cat

the tattered chair
in front of the computer
where you invited every virus
with your reckless searching

—
tonight a full moon rises
up behind the cedars

I roam from room to room—

Lament

The August beach is as you left it:
hung with absconding shadows
across the afternoon

the sun moving south
over horizon islands

yellow jackets busy in the sand
mining the detritus
in the line of seaweed the tide left.

No agates or feathers call to me today,
as they did to you always,
just the rattle of colored stones—
the greens and greys, whites and golds
shifting under my sandals

and the piercing squawks of seagulls
over a herring ball in the bay.

Out of summer's perfect
and lonely afternoon,
a moment returns to me from long ago.

Taking your hand as we moved
in a festival crowd
I let fall away
every contentious word
every argument, letting go
purely into the love you offered—

Did I give you what you needed
in the end?

Ritual

Shrine of driftwood plinths
embedded at the top of the beach:
rocks and shells in wave patterns,
in circles and spirals,
for days we have built this,
added to it—
eagle feathers stuck into the sand
as you would place
each walk's find.

This evening, stacking driftwood
in a crisscrossed tower,
your son builds a pyre.

He mounds dried seaweed
and shavings of beach cedar,
adds sawdust from your shop,
scraps of your work jeans, what
essence we could find, and
a cigarette from your stash.

After we pour your ashes
into the lip of the tide,
watch them dissolve in a white wave,
after we sift them onto the sand
around shells and feathers,
we each strike a match.

As the pyre flames up
and caves in on itself,
we pour the last ash in

while out of thick cloud cover,
the bright disc of sun
drops down
to blaze the shoreline,
answering
the glow of the collapsing tower.

Sunset grows deeper,
more golden, a muted neon
from western sky to water sheen
its pinks and peaches
its blue shimmers over silver
spreading in the rhythm
of lapping tide,

> this shore where you would
> each night exclaim,
> *we are so lucky*

until the faint light in the west fades
and the beach is lit only
by the sea's face,
its luminescent
grey.

Sunday

I woke and felt again the deep
hollow of the house.

The young cat slept on in her corner chair,
her sister's mounded weight at my side.

The day grew light and blossomed
from every window. Hours passed.

I cleaned the kitchen, brushed
the crumbs off the floor, emptied

dried flowers from the blue vase.
Once or twice a wave of grief

swept over me, burning the corners of my eyes,
as I walked by the pictures on the shelf.

I lived next to your absence all afternoon:
this hard apprenticeship at love's last lesson.

Eight Months

This morning I turned on my left side,
reaching out to feel again the taut, warm skin
over your ribs, the round moles along your side,
the humming furnace of your heart.

I could almost smell your musk,
tobacco, sun, and cabernet—
sweet ghost, thin companion.

On my phone I find you alive and
pensive in your chair, oxygen cannula
translucent against your drawn face,
your eyes losing their light.

Cold morning air drops over me
as I let the cats out into the yard.
They race to climb the *pieris,*
heavy with its white bells
ringing against the dark fence.

PechaKucha for Michael

[island]

When I tell our story I will say
I found you to bring you here:
to this small cliff above the beach
with its clinging trees—
kingfisher's branch and eagle's snag—
to these spavined rocks the grandchildren
love to climb, flowing down to packed sand,
to this clearing in an abandoned orchard
where we built summer's house.
Mornings we took our coffee to the yard
where the first sun warmed the grass.

[bedspread]

Under the billowing Indian bedspread
pinned to the ceiling of the small
back bedroom in your tumbled-down
duplex where we first lived—green and red
elephants marching across a yellow background—
I'd wake those mornings thinking:
what luxury! this love! We can have
this lovemaking for the rest of our lives.

[valentine]

The heft of the silver heart you gave me
resting in red tissue
in its small wooden box
stamped, *fragile* seems now to say
everything you couldn't
about your pain.

[burning]

As you grew older, you couldn't stop
telling your parents' story: your father
in Buchenwald, saved by the money
his first wife raised to buy him out;
your mother, a courier for the underground,
arrested in Italy. You and your sister born
in Rome. The letters your father wrote
to Truman asking for asylum.
In 1967, you burned your draft card
in the university stadium.

[old fir]

It leans out from the bank, carved
and curved by a thousand winter storms,
traversing the crumbling clay,
it hangs on, last outpost of the forest
over the shifting cobble.

[red boat]

You'd take the rusted bone-handled knife
out to the buoy to cut away the winter's growth
of kelp and seaweed from the lines,
bobbing in the red inflatable,
working the tangled rope until the buoy
floated higher, relieved of its weight.

[seal]

On summer nights in the bay,
always there is one sentinel seal

patrolling the shore, its grey skull
just breaking the oily silk waves of twilight.
Watching us around the beach fire,
it drifts into the dark: totem, talisman,
memento mori.

[table]

From the wide trunk of the double cedar
that almost took out our roof
as it twisted coming down,
you have measured and planed
wide planks for a dining room table.
Days in your shop, fitting and smoothing it,
fashioning a base that will hold it:
perseverance furthers, you say.

[feathers]

You know where to find them: at the high tide line
under the trees where the eagles land.
Soaking in the sun as you lean against a drift log,
you've marked their soaring trajectories.

[summer dust]

Found the mound of work jeans piled in the corner
still heavy with sawdust and dirt,
pockets packed with butts and bent nails,
denim stiff with stains from lacquer, paint
and wine. You loved to make things, make a mess,
find the beauty in the wood. You never
painted the sheet-rocked walls of your shop.

[ashtray]

I place again the morning kiss
on your bent neck as you rest
your cigarette on the lip of the fireplace
trying to coax the smoke up the chimney,
and I feel such tenderness
even out of the rage:
you didn't take care of yourself.

[agates]

You see them slant, have honed the vision
to pick them out of the millions
of white and gold stones on the beach.
Hold them to the sun to see their translucence.

[each day]

To say what living's for—
to move through sorrow, anger,
even despair, to find again
the center where I love you
for your poet soul, behind smoke-wrinkled
skin, your faulty ears, your whitening hair—-

[black box]

Inside: wafers of ash
placed on the tongue
of the tide, falling
in the glamour
of summer waters,
tossed where currents

swirl spindrift foam
in the bay.
Your grave and grace
will be return
at the edge
of the circling sea.

[new year's eve]

Now we must put away the old year—
the year that last contained you,
your life and death year.

In the night the cat comes to your side of the bed.
She rasps her rough tongue along my arm
and curls there to take up the missing-ness:
rough knobs of your backbone,
sun-tanned shoulders,
elegant curve of your head,
deep comfort of being mated.

Triad

Sometimes I can almost grasp
a moment from the long dance
of distance and intimacy,

the push-pull of what I loved
in you and what I could not abide—
(Does anyone love wholly,

without reserve?) I loved
your face, its Roman marble
symmetry, your wide brow,

your deep tenderness.
But mostly I lived contained
alongside the solitude in you:

as the hull of a red boat
skims on top of the dark,
hidden pull of the tide,

as two trees across a meadow
leafing out toward each other
collude with clouds.

The flowering world can't hold me
or the coolness of the grass
under the mock orange.

It takes flesh to honor flesh,
and even memory cannot
bring back the embrace

under the skylight stars,
the turned heat of your back
in the summer bed.

First of July

The fire sets the wood stove rustling,
its tiny song in the quiet house,
while small rock hammers of rain
tap onto the wooden deck.

Maple, alder, and hemlock are leafing
hard to close the hole of light
in the clearing. Mower, scythe,
and chainsaw keep it open.

Where is memory's sharpened blade?
I fear I am losing you entirely:
your scent, your dry laugh, your sighs
covered over with a season's weeds.

Not a breath of wind in the wet
clearing. Just green, green light
and the damp grey
sheen of the soaked deck.

Midsummer

these summer mornings   the trees
seem to be waiting for a revelation

while the sunrise quietly
composes the blue behind them

last night the sunset was a bust   a too-much brightness
and then gone   little color along horizon islands

we fed the beach fire old wood and waited
for the comet to show   it never did

I pushed the emptied wheelbarrow up the hill

Iris walked ahead with the flashlight
pointing out tripping roots in the road

The cat was at the door watching a moth batter the glass

Sand spilled from the cuffs of my jeans when I undressed

I slipped into sleep and woke
in an unknown day

a spill of white daisies in the sun
and the trees   alert again to the mourning—

Bequeath

I bequeath you the house your grandfather built,
its dry shingles and fading grey trim.

Bequeath you the clearing, early flurry of birds
in the weed trees: white fir and maple intruding on the light.

Bequeath you the wide yard of grass
and the finicky mower,

the apples, the blueberries,
the grafted plum that never bears,

the well and water tank,
the black generator spewing exhaust.

Bequeath you the shed's clutter of tools and useful junk
under powder-post beetles' small piles of sawdust,

the chainsaw in its orange case,
its rusty teeth and special file.

Bequeath you the trail to the beach
and the August ground wasps' ambush,

the tent platform and sunset bench,
boards slowly sinking into the mossy bluff,

the red, rubber boat and its bellows pump,
the blue truck weighted with sandbags against spring mud.

Bequeath you summer days on a low-tide beach,
eagle feathers and agates, barnacles and muck.

Bequeath you the midnight sky in June, its smear of stars,
old chaos of carbon and the given light.

In the Clearing

I lie down now in the clearing we carved
from the forest opening, the woods a protective
gate around us. Womb of darkness,
root of silence. Towhees scratch in dry salal.

Where you built our house in sunlit woods,
above thickets of blackberry, thimbleberry, nettle,
the mother tree curves a hundred years
out of her charred gashes.

As my dream foretold, we move in a luminous room.
Borage and cornflower rise with their sheen of dust,
an abandoned orchard whitens on lichened limbs,
and fallen logs, moss-covered, soften into duff.

Through the trees, night tide's deep throb.
Starlight pours into a dark bowl. Fiery
islands shine behind the palisade of night.

Lie down now in the clearing.
In the womb of darkness.
Love built this house.

ACKNOWLEDGMENTS

Some of these poems first appeared in the following publications:

The Madrona Project, vol. 2: "World Without Us"

Cirque: "The Grounding Line"

Lights, Pleasure Boat Studio: "Gathering," "Reunion," "Blueprint"

Pontoon: "Eclipsed"

Balancing Acts: "Side by Side"

Stealing Light, Raven Chronicles Anthology: "The Iceman"

Last Call: "In the Anthropocene"

Terrain.org: "Beauty Resists"

Floating Bridge Review (2008 – 2015): "Alongside Her Dying," "November Fragments," "Sitting with Iris," "In the Vale of Soul-Making," "To Tao Chi'en"

Metro Poetry Bus: "Fulcrum"

Exhibition: "At Griffin Bay"

Upstream: "Listening to the Sea at Pt. Wilson"

Yalapaloosa Review: "Teaching Homer to Eighth Graders"

Insistent in the Skin, Brooding Heron Press chapbook: "Fulcrum," "Scars," "Fierce"

Deep gratitude to poet friends whose responses helped make this collection stronger: Lise Goett, for her vision and expert help shaping the manuscript; Sherry Rind, Mercedes Lawry, Anne Pitkin, Eileen Duncan, writing group companions; Samuel Green for all the years of sharing, debate, and support; Ed Harkness, so generous with his attention to the details of individual poems; Michael Turnsen, first reader, deeply missed.

The Community of Writers at Squaw Valley has been a source of encouragement and solidarity over the years. Special thanks to Brenda Hillman and Bob Hass for inspiration and long friendship. I am grateful to Jim Moore for his mentorship through the Split Rock Arts Program. The Lakeside School provided support for a sabbatical year and for summer writing retreats during which some of these poems were written.

Every writer should be blessed to have readers who are always eager for the latest poems: Margy Ligon, Ilse Turnsen, Pamela Mills—thank you.

Photo by John Ligon

A native of Seattle, **ALICIA HOKANSON** grew up exploring the beaches, forests, and islands of Puget Sound, inspiring her deep attention to the natural world.

Her first book, *Mapping the Distance,* was selected by Carolyn Kizer for the King County Arts Commission publication prize and it was released by Breitenbush Books in 1989. Brooding Heron Press published two chapbooks, *Phosphorous* and *Insistent in the Skin.* Her poems have appeared in a wide variety of journals and anthologies.

Upon completing her B.A. and M.A. in English at the University of Washington, Alicia pursued a career teaching English in a variety of venues, from working with high-school students in South Australia to teaching grades 1-8 in a one-room schoolhouse on Waldron Island, 8th graders on Bainbridge Island, and middle-school English for 27 years at Lakeside School in Seattle. Named *River of Words* Poetry Teacher of the year in 2003 for her work nurturing young writers, she also held the Bleakney Chair in English at Lakeside upon her retirement in 2014.

She now devotes her time to writing, reading, and advocating for social and environmental justice.